BLANK PAGE

Index

BLANK PAGE

Introduction

Did you know that **people with exceptional abilities can apply for a special visa and live in the United States of America?** If you are an athlete, an artist, a multinational executive or manager, a professor or researcher, if you have a PhD, have done something relevant or are an above average person in your country, you can be one of those people!

You do not need a lawyer or a process manager to apply for an extraordinary abilities Visa (EB VISA), **you can do it by yourself**. All you have to do is compile the data and write your process! After all, **who better than you to know every aspect of your life and be able to explain what you have accomplished that is most significant and relevant!?**

Of course, presenting a good and strong process for the authorities in the United States of America to recognize your worth and why you deserve to **"get a pass" to live the American dream is essential!**

This book aims to serve as **a guide to help you prepare your self-petition** and be able to achieve the American dream!

In this book you will find everything you'll need to prepare your application for an Extraordinary People Visa (EB Visa), including a step-by-step guide and a copy of the entire process from who already done it, so that you have no doubts and have a winning application.

What is an EB1?

Extraordinary Ability (EB1) Green card stands for Employment Based Immigration visa first preference category, often known as a preferred category for permanent residency in the United States of America. These are foreign people with exceptional abilities, great academics, or researchers, as well as some executives and managers from international companies who have been transferred to the United States.

An EB1A petition's beneficiary must qualify as an "Alien of extraordinary ability". The United States Citizenship and Immigration Services (USCIS) defines extraordinary ability as a "level of expertise indicating that the individual is one of those few who have risen to the top of the field of endeavor."

There are two ways to demonstrate exceptional ability. The first way is to demonstrate that the person is a recipient of a globally renowned and well-recognized award. The second way is to demonstrate that the beneficiary meets three of the ten USCIS criteria for extraordinary ability. Three of these must be met as a minimum; however, this does not ensure approval.

The second way is a two-part examination in EB1A, in which the applicant must first meet at least three of the ten following listed USCIS regulatory requirements for EB1A;

1. Receipt of lesser national or international prizes or awards for excellence in their field of endeavor;

2. Membership in associations in the field of endeavor that require outstanding achievements of their members;

3. Published material about the alien and his work in professional journals, trade publications, or the major media;

4. Participation, either in a group or alone, as a judge of others in the same or a similar field;

5. Original scientific, scholarly, or artistic contributions of major significance in the field of endeavor;

6. Authorship of scholarly articles in the field, published in professional journals or the major media;

7. Display of the alien's work at artistic exhibitions or showcases in more than one country;

8. Performance in a lead, starring, or critical role for organizations with a distinguished reputation;

9. Commanding a high salary compared to others in the field; or

10. Commercial success in the performing arts, as shown by box office receipts and sales.

And then their merits are evaluated based on the following two criteria:

i.   Petitioner is one of the small percentages of people who have risen to the very top of the field of endeavor.
ii.   Sustained national or international acclaim and that his or her achievements have been recognized in the field of expertise.

When you work on unique challenges that need interdisciplinary skills, you are unquestionably at the top of your area. You should plan and present your case from the standpoint that the combination of interdisciplinary abilities required to complete your PhD is exceptional in its own terms, and that you belong to the small fraction of people who have reached the top of your field. You should have well-known specialists in each discipline submit reference letters indicating that you are at the top of your multidisciplinary field of study.

It becomes easier to demonstrate that you have maintained national or international recognition if you have at least three years of study or professional experience beyond your PhD. In this case, you would have publications with a large number of citations spread out across a long period of time, and the number of citations would be gradually increasing over time. Citations might be interpreted as evidence of peer review approval. As a result, citations spread out over a few years are a reliable indicator of long-term acclaim. You should get letters from people who have benefited from your work. These letters have the ability to convey long-term acclaim.

Any proof that demonstrates how the Extraordinary Ability applicant's admission will benefit the United States or is of national importance will be beneficial. It is essential that you add a few elements that establish this link and demonstrate how the permanent status granted under the employment-based category helps the United States.

To summarize, you should be aware that the points 1-10 above, as well as the "very top of the field" criteria, must be prioritized. However, it is OK to emphasize that your extraordinary qualities will benefit the United States.

If your work helps or enhances the following, it can be considered beneficial to the United States:

1) improves the economy of the United States;
2) improves wages and working conditions for Americans;
3) aids educational and training initiatives for youngsters and underqualified workers in the United States;
4) provide more affordable housing for Americans who are young, old, or poor;
5) improves the environment in the United States and leads to more efficient use of the country's resources;
6) contributes to national security;
7) it is a key or strategic technology area that the government agency has recognized;
8) it is a significant technological area with the potential to have a significant influence;
9) contributes to defense research;
10) it is fundamental research with wide range of national applications.

In general, most thesis work will benefit the United States in some way. Most funding agencies designate funding areas based on criterion that benefit the United States. As a result, if your research is financed by a government agency, it is extremely probable that it fits within one of these strategic research areas that will be helpful to the United States in the long run. You can utilize parts of the US government agencies circulars, which are available online and describe how their operations help the nation, in your petition. If you can figure out which strategic area your study supports, you can figure out where you fit into the bigger picture and how your work benefits the US.

Can I apply by myself?

Most people hire a lawyer for this process because they believe that a lawyer will be most successful and efficient in obtaining permanent status. However, in self-petitioning categories such as EB1 and EB2, the applicant ends up doing the majority of the work for the lawyer. The strength of the petition in these two categories is determined by the strength of the supporting evidence, and the rest of the petition is based on this evidence. This book seeks to relieve you of the burden of worrying about the strategy and time spent writing the petition itself, allowing you to focus on gathering evidence for the application. You may just assemble all the information and present it as a plausible statement in the petition, just like a lawyer.

You are best prepared to successfully tell your narrative and how your current and future work can be considered extraordinary or how it will help the nation if you believe your work is in the US national interest or can be deemed part of Extraordinary Ability.

You've previously prepared an original research thesis that you believe is of national importance or demonstrates your exceptional ability; you must be capable of producing a rich and faultless document with all the essential supporting evidence.

Step by step for preparing the petition

You will be able to file for an I-140 without having to go through the labor certification process if you are self-petitioning for a green card through EB1A or the National Interest Wavier Program (NIW). As a result, filing an EB1A self-petition will spare you the trouble and time involved with the labor certification process. In general, to apply for a green card under the self-petition EB1A-EA and EB2-NIW categories, you must undertake two steps.

The I-140 form is the initial step toward permanent residency. The I-140 form is used to request to USCIS for permanent residency eligibility. Approval of the I-140 does not make you a permanent resident; your status remains non-immigrant as long as you have a valid visa; rather, it allows you to adjust your status to permanent residence if a visa number becomes available. In general, there are no annual limits on the number of I-140 permits given. The requirements for gaining approval for an EB1A petition can be found on the USCIS website.

It is possible to file a self-petition I-140 application at any moment. A complete I-140 application consists of a I-140 application form, application fee, petition requesting permanent residency from a USCIS examiner, recommendation letters, and other supporting documents. The time it takes for an I-140 petition to be approved can range from a few weeks to many months. The USCIS website has current processing times for I-140 approval that vary by filing location and filing category.

Even if you seek green cards for everyone in your family, you only need to file one I-140 application. The primary applicant is the individual who files the I-140, and derivative applicants are those who are qualified to file I-485 adjustment of status applications and other related benefit applications.

The following documents should be included in your I-140 petition to USCIS:

a) Petition cover letter
b) I-140 Immigrant petition for Alien Worker, with filing fee (At the time of filing, you should download a new application file and follow the instructions for the current application fee.)
c) Photocopy certification
d) Legal documents of petitioner residence (photocopy of latest I-94; H1B visa, and I-797A, notice of approval of H1B status; all immigration paperwork' historical records; IAP-66, J1 approval notice, or DS-2019: certificate of eligibility for exchange visitor (J-1) status; photocopy of relevant pages from passport; copy of social security card)
e) Petition for Extraordinary Ability under extraordinary ability
f) Statement of Beneficiary on Work Plans in the United States
g) List of Evidences
h) Evidences

The application for status adjustment is the second step (I-485). To change your existing non-immigrant status to permanent resident status, you must complete an adjustment of status application. The approval of I-485 is the final step in the application process, and once approved, you should receive a green card. Applying for an I-485 involves filling the application form, I-485 application fee, photocopies of immigration visa records, birth certificate, biometric fee, employment records, statement of work plans, and optional travel document and employment authorization applications if needed. A I-485 application is required for each member of your family who seeks to receive a green card. They can also submit an I-765 or I-131 application if needed.

We recommend that you first review your educational, career, and employment history. Create a precise timeline of all significant events in your education and professional life. After that, gather evidence for all the items on your lists. Education certificates, corporate certifications attesting your outstanding work in the field, reference letters, peer review reports, publications about you in relevant journals, citation reports, and so on are examples. With the help of this book and the time you set aside for strategy and writing, you'll be able to spend the majority of your time gathering evidence for an effective petition.

As previously stated, the purpose of this book is to relieve you of the stress of worrying about the strategy and time spent composing the petition, and the completion of forms is part of the process organization. You should concentrate on gathering and organizing all of the evidence that will support your petition. This evidence is added to the main petition as exhibits and is organized such that it can be easily referenced in the main petition.

Following is a list of the most frequent types of evidence that may be applicable to your case:

a) Awards.
b) Academic degrees, certificates.

c) Abstract of your MSc and PhD thesis work.
d) Schools and their national and international standing.
e) Reference letters (proving your extraordinary ability in the field, It's a good idea to choose referees who are experts in your field or who use the work you're arguing for EB1A. It's even better if the references come from different countries.).
f) Past and present jobs if relevant for the field.
g) Conference talks, invited talks, invitation letters for events or peer reviews, Information on participation in panels as a judge of others in the field.
h) Copy of your publications including at last the title page, impact factors of journals in which you published and number of article downloads. Journal citation records of your publications (Google scholar, ResearchGate, Academic institutions and others).
i) Articles you reviewed, request for review from journal editors, criteria for selection of journal reviewer-ship, thank you letters from technical editors of journals you acted as a reviewer or copies of review reports, if available.
j) Project reports you authored or co-authored, abstracts of proposals funded, and evidence of funding received.
k) Membership of professional associations and requirements for membership when relevant to the field.
l) Patents, provisional patents, and invention disclosures, innovation or research work being used by peers or private industry or federal labs. Information pertaining to your research area and its national importance.

Auxiliary information

USCIS website: http://www.uscis.gov

USCIS case status: https://egov.uscis.gov

Visa Bulletin: http://travel.state.gov

Petition template

COVER LETTER

USCIS   From,
Attn: I-140   Mr _____
Address _____   Address _____
_____   _____

RE: EB1A-Extraordinary Ability Petition for Lawful Permanent Residency.
Petitioner/Beneficiary: Dr. _____, Ph.D. (Self)
Classification Sought: 203(b)(1)(A)
Type of Petition: I-140

Dear Examiner

Please find enclosed:

- G-1145 Form

- I-140 Form

- Bank International Money Order with $_____ fee

- Photocopy Certification

- Copy of passport

- Petition for EB1- Extraordinary Ability

- Table of Evidence Vs Exhibits

- Exhibits Index

- Exhibits

Thank you very much for your responsiveness.

Best regards,

_____, PhD

G-1145 Form

https://www.uscis.gov/sites/default/files/document/forms/g-1145.pdf

I-140 Form

https://www.uscis.gov/sites/default/files/document/forms/i-140.pdf

Photocopy Certification

Dear Examiner

The petitioner, _____, Passport Number _____, certify that the attached documents, ahead designated as exhibits, and the duplicate retained by me are true, exact, complete, and unaltered photocopies made by me.

_____, _____, 20____.

_____

Your Name

PETITION FOR EXTRAORDINARY ABILITY

USCIS
Attn: I-140
Address_____
_____

From,
Mr _____
Address _____
_____

RE: EB1A-Extraordinary Ability Petition for Lawful Permanent Residency.
Petitioner/Beneficiary: Dr. _____, Ph.D. (Self)
Classification Sought: 203(b)(1)(A)
Type of Petition: I-140

Dear Examiner:

The following evidence is respectfully submitted in support of Dr. _____ (Ph.D.) petition to be classified as a qualified immigrant under the preference of alien of extraordinary ability professional. This evidence will specifically demonstrate that Dr._____ qualifies for the classification 203(b)(1)(A) as an extraordinary ability alien due to the following reasons.

I. Dr. _____ is a known expert in the field of _____ with over ____ years of research expertise in the specific area of _____. For the following grounds, Dr. _____ qualifies as an alien of extraordinary ability. (Please see Sections 1, 2, 3 and 4).

    a. Dr. _____ has received an award for the national interest in his field of research (Please see Section 1 [G]).

    b. Dr. _____ is member of associations in the field of _____ that require outstanding achievements of their members (Please see Section 1 [C]).

    c. Dr. _____ research work was published in national scientific media. (Please see Section 1 [I]).

    d. Dr. _____ has individually participated as a judge of the work of others in the same or an allied field of specialization for which classification is sought; (Please see Section 1 [H]).

e. Dr. _____ has original scientific research that are of major significance in the field of _____ and are also expected to benefit United States; (Please see Section 1 [E], Section 1 [F], Section 2, Section 3 and Section 4).

f. Dr. _____ has authorship of numerous scholarly articles in the field, in internationally recognized professional publications; (Please see Section 1 [E], Section 1 [F] and Section 2).

g. Dr. _____ has had his work exposed in several national and international events (Please see Section 1 [J]).

h. Dr. _____ has performed in a leading role for organizations that have a distinguished reputation. (Please see Section 1, [D]).

II. Dr. _____ is one of the small percentages risen to the top of the interdisciplinary field of _____ (Please see Section 1 [A], Section 1 [B] and Section 2).

III. Dr. _____ work has sustained acclaim by international researchers. (Please see Section 1 [A], Section 1 [B], Section 1 [E], Section 1[F], Section 2 and Section 3).

IV. Dr. _____ seeks work in the area of _____, an area of which has substantial inherent value and national importance for the United States. (Please see Section 1 [A], Section 1 [B], Section 2 and Section 4).

Section 1: Dr. _____ is an alien of extraordinary ability and is a recognized top specialist in the interdisciplinary field of _____ with over _____ years research experience in the exact area of _____. Dr. _____ accomplishments are well-documented.

[A] Dr. _____ possesses advanced degrees from famous institutions. His qualifications are unique as compared to other researchers in the field.

The petitioner owns a bachelor's degree in _____ obtained at University _____ at _____ in _____ (Please see exhibit E2.3). To obtain the bachelor's degree he presented a monograph on the subject of _____ (Please see exhibit E6.3). In _____ Dr. _____ ended his Master in _____ held at the University of _____ in _____ (Please see exhibit E2.2), with the thesis "_____" (Please see exhibit E6.2). Dr. _____ obtained is PhD in _____ at the University of _____ in _____ (Please see exhibit E2.1) with the thesis "_____" (Please see exhibit E6.1). In addition to his academic qualifications, Dr. _____ has been increasing his knowledge through training in a highly specialized area such as the areas of _____ (Please see exhibit E1, E2.4 and E2.5).

[B] Dr. _____ has in-depth knowledge of the area of _____ and is recognized as a top expert in this field. His expertise in this field is considered extraordinary.

"Dr. _____ work, is pioneering in the field of _____, being the first to address scientifically the study of the _____. Thus the results and the methodologies developed by Dr. _____ for _____ related research are mandatory for any researcher working in this topic" (Please see exhibit E3.8, letter from _____, University of _____).

"_____ has evidenced an impressive motivation and performance that, in my opinion, constitute a clear guarantee of his intellectual capacities and abilities to carry out high quality research in his future career" (Please see exhibit E3.2, letter from Dr. _____, University of _____).

"His professional life has remained in the same path of searching for solutions, either by application of techniques already known and consolidated, as by innovation and development, ensuring the permanent updating of knowledge, along with the best and latest technological and market practices." (Please see exhibit E3.6, letter from _____, Company _____).

"I am confident that Dr. _____ will continue to display excellent academic performance. I expect Mr. _____ to respond to the challenge of _____ program with a rigorous devotion to excellence. Aside from his outstanding academic qualities, Dr. _____ has a wealth of academic experience. Dr. _____ can bring a unique viewpoint, combined with an awareness and familiarity with the international world. He offers all the qualities of a good leader, and all of the characteristics desirable in an ideal team member." (Please see exhibit E3.4, letter from Dr. _____, _____ University).

"Dr. _____ is a topmost researcher in his field, where he can have further contribution for the development of the state of art anywhere in the world." (Please see exhibit E3.3, letter from Dr. _____, University of _____).

[C] Dr. _____ is a member of prestigious national society.

Dr. _____ is an effective member of the "_____" in _____. The "_____" is the _____. Under the _____ law, and namely the provisions of _____, the "_____" is duly empowered to attribute the title of _____ and to regulate the practice of the _____ profession (Please see Exhibit E4.5). Dr. _____ holds a professional license being licensed to practice _____ in _____ (Please see Exhibit E4.5).

Between the period _____ to _____, Dr. _____ was a research member of the ▮▮▮▮▮▮▮▮▮▮ (Please see exhibit E4.2). The ▮▮▮▮▮▮▮▮▮▮ is a research unit funded by the ▮▮▮▮▮▮▮▮▮▮, incorporating ▮▮▮▮▮▮▮▮▮▮. In the last Research Assessment Exercise (20__-20__) that was recently announced (▮▮▮▮▮), the research institution was rated as ▮▮▮▮▮. The Unit is organized in ▮▮▮▮▮ Research Groups, addressing the topics of ▮▮▮▮▮▮▮▮▮▮. The work developed by Dr. ▮▮▮▮▮ in this institution focused on ▮▮▮▮▮▮▮▮. In short, the research institution aims at promoting innovation and sustainability, with a close link to the ▮▮▮▮▮▮▮▮ (Please see exhibits E4.2).

[D] Dr. ▮▮▮▮▮ has performed in a leading role for various projects in organizations that have distinguished reputation.

Dr. ▮▮▮▮▮ has large experience of ▮▮▮▮▮ in the ▮▮▮▮▮. During the years ▮▮▮ to ▮▮▮ Dr. ▮▮▮▮▮ had a leading role at ▮▮▮▮▮▮▮▮ where he developed his ▮▮▮▮▮ activities, namely in the leadership of the ▮▮▮▮▮ (Please see exhibits E4.4, E3.4, E3.6, E3.7 and E1).

"Timely and abiding by the established deadlines, he also showed the capacity to take on the role of leader of a team towards high performance and productivity. Its dynamism and natural optimism, without loss of sense of reality, have helped to overcome the objectives and obstacles that have been proposed or are emerging, being a man of solutions and not of problems (one of the fundamental characteristics in a co-worker, in my best opinion)" (Please see exhibit E3.6, letter from ▮▮▮▮▮▮▮▮▮▮, company▮▮▮▮▮▮▮).

During the period ▮▮▮ to ▮▮▮, Dr. ▮▮▮▮▮ developed research at ▮▮▮▮▮▮▮▮▮▮, working on the field of ▮▮▮▮▮▮▮▮ (Please see exhibits E4.2, E3.1, E3.2, E3.3 and E3.8).

Between the years of ▮▮▮ and ▮▮▮, Dr. ▮▮▮▮▮ developed research under the project ▮▮▮▮▮▮▮▮ at the ▮▮▮▮▮ (Please see exhibit E4.1). _____ project addressed the query related with the _____. The project findings become a helpful instrument to identify _____ (Please see exhibits E6.4).

Since _____, Dr. _____ contributes as a reviewer in his area of expertise for the _____ (Please see exhibit E5.1).

[E] His knowledge and contributions to this field are invaluable and have impacted this area of study greatly.

In the course of his career, Dr. _____ has demonstrated outstanding expertise in _____, particularly as it relates to the _____. Dr. _____ has employed his strong expertise to make multiple major contributions in his field. In both his doctoral research and post-doctoral research, Dr. _____ has been carrying out remarkable research. He has performed pioneering research on the topic of _____ (Please see exhibits E3.1, E3.2, E3.8, E6.1 and E7.8), and made a critical development in _____ in Country_____ (Please see exhibits E6.4, E7.6 and E7.7). He has played a critical and pivotal role in several projects that have generated numerous contributions reported in books and prestigious journals (Please see exhibits E7 and E8). The influence of Dr. _____ published works can be seen in the fact that his work has been cited frequently by other scientists in prestigious national and international journals and conferences (Please see exhibits E7).

[F] Dr. _____ has widely published in this field and has presented at several international recognized conferences.

In the last _____ years, Dr. _____ was able to publish _____ books (Please see Exhibit E7.5 and E7.6), _____ chapter of a book (Please see exhibit E.7.7) and approximately _____ papers in international journals and conference proceedings on the topic of _____, wish acknowledge him before other researchers in the field (Please see exhibits E7, E8 and E1).

"Dr. _____ demonstrated a high level of autonomy, creativity, motivation and diligence, which resulted in progresses in his research and in the publication of relevant results in leading international journals and conferences" (Please see exhibit E3.1, letter from Dr. _____, University of _____).

[G] Dr. _____ has received an award by the _____ for the national interest in his research field.

In the year _____, Dr. _____ was awarded with a _____ from the _____ (Please see exhibit E4.3). Proposals to the _____ are evaluated by a jury specifically set for this call based on the field of _____. Applicants are awarded grades from _____ to _____, for each of the following criteria; _____. Applicants are ranked according to weighted average of the scores for each criterion. In the year of _____, the year when Dr. _____ was awarded, were submitted _____ applications and _____ applicants were awarded, considering all areas of scientific knowledge at national level (Please see exhibits E4.3).

[H] Dr. _____ has acted as a referee and reviewer for high impact international journals and international conferences.

Since _____, Dr. _____ is a reviewer in his area of expertise for the _____ (Please see exhibit E5.1). "_____ provides a multidisciplinary forum for dissemination of practice-based information on the _____ issues concerning all aspects of _____. Peer-reviewed papers and case studies will address issues and topics related to _____, such as _____" (Please see exhibit E5.1). The _____ from the _____ as an RG impact factor of _____ and an H Index of _____ (Please see exhibits E5.1).

In _____, Dr. _____ was referee in the international scientific committee of the International Conference on _____ that was organized in _____ in _____ (Please see exhibit E5.2).

[I] The work that Dr. ▆▆▆▆ has developed was mentioned in major scientific media.

Dr. ▆▆▆▆▆ work was mentioned in ▆▆▆▆ , 20▆▆ in the ▆▆▆▆▆▆▆▆▆▆▆▆ . The ▆▆▆▆▆▆▆▆▆▆▆▆▆▆ covers the main activities developed from ▆▆▆▆▆▆▆▆▆▆ . In this edition are mentioned ▆▆▆ national ▆▆▆ projects, and ▆▆▆▆▆ research work being the research work of Dr. ▆▆▆▆▆ one of the works mentioned (Please see exhibit E8.1). Dr. ▆▆▆▆▆ book entitled "▆▆▆▆▆▆▆▆▆▆▆▆▆▆▆▆" is mentioned in several bookstores of various countries around the world (Please see exhibits E7.5).

[J] Dr. ▆▆▆▆▆ research was present in several exhibitions in different countries.

The research work developed by Dr. ▆▆▆▆▆ has been presented in numerous national and international exhibitions. In ▆▆▆▆▆ the work developed by Dr. ▆▆▆▆▆ was present on an exhibition in ▆▆▆▆▆▆▆▆▆▆▆▆▆▆▆ (Please see exhibit E8.2). Dr. ▆▆▆▆▆ work has been present in exhibitions in several countries in world (four samples are showed in exhibits E8.3). His work and publications are displayed in the repositories of renowned universities such as the University of ▆▆▆▆▆▆▆▆▆ (Please see exhibits E7.3 and E7.4).

Section 2: Dr. _____ is one of the small percentage risen to the very top of the interdisciplinary field of _____.

Dr. _____ knowledge and contributions to the field of _____ are invaluable to this research field. His work has already impacted this area and holds many future promises. It is abundantly clear that Dr. _____ has produced original scientific contributions that have significantly influenced his field. He has truly established himself as an outstanding professional in his field.

"The candidate shows a good scientific production which can be placed within the contest of _____. This has a well-established discipline of _____ studies. His scientific production is characterized by a remarkable interdisciplinary by embracing typical _____ issues such as _____, etc. The theoretical background of his research is very wide embracing different areas" (Please see exhibit E3.1, letter from Dr. _____, _____ University).

"Mr. _____ experimented the use of new advanced _____ for _____ applications and _____. The results of his studies contributed a lot to the knowledge of _____" (Please see exhibit E3.5, letter from Dr. _____, University of _____).

Dr. _____ possesses unique and innovative skills, knowledge, and background that serve the national interest and cannot be easily replaced. As can be seen from his remarkable accomplishments, Dr. _____ has highly valuable skills for the United States. In addition to his technical expertise, Dr. _____ is distinguished through special traits like his uncommon intellect and work ethic (Please see exhibits E3). Certainly, such factors are beyond the scope of a labor certification process. All of his special skills, abilities, and knowledge combined with his past record of success make Dr. _____ ideally suited to serve the national interests of United States. Moreover, these unique traits of his cannot be articulated in a labor certification process.

"He has shown excellent classroom management skills and developed a rapport with

students and colleagues that is characterized by mutual respect; he is charismatic and creative, and he thinks outside the box. _____ also demonstrated a deep commitment in his individual assignments and high methodological and scientific abilities, particularly on the scope of _____"
(Please see exhibit E3.7, letter from Dr. _____, University _____).

"Has a professional and colleague, I can say that Dr. _____ shows an extremely high level of professionalism, visible by his very honest behavior of high ethical standards, either with trainees, colleagues and superiors, from very small to very sensitive or important tasks. Due to our close working relation, I can say that Dr. _____ is high responsible person, able to oversee complex research teams or of large projects" (Please see exhibit E3.8, letter from Dr. _____, University of _____).

Section 3: Dr. _____ work has sustained acclaim by international researchers.

[A] Dr. _____ has an impressive record of success that has sustained interest and is well recognized by experts and used widely by many researchers in the field nationally and internationally. His work has considerable impact on his field as evidenced using his research results by others in high impact journals.

According to Google Scholar, Dr. _____ publications have been cited ____ times since 20__ (Please see exhibits E7.1). Dr. _____ publications in ResearchGate have been cited ____ times and read _____ times (Please see exhibits E7.1). Dr. _____ first publication, with the title "_____" was, according to Google Scholar, the most cited publication with ____ citations (Please see exhibit E7.1).

Dr. _____ scientific article entitled "_____" published in the high impact journal "_____" has been widely cited (Please see exhibits E7.8). According to Google Scholar this article was cited ____ times (Please see exhibit E7.1), according to the ResearchGate this article was cited ____ times (Please see exhibit E7.8) and according with the Scopus preview from _____ this article was cited ____ times in _____ Journals.

Dr. _____ is one of the authors of the book "_____" that was published in 20__. This book was based on the research developed in his latest research project and has had more than _____ downloads from ____ countries (Please see exhibits E7.6). It is also important and relevant to highlight that Dr. _____ book entitled "_____" is on sale in several bookstores of various countries around the world (Please see exhibits E7.5).

[B] Dr. _____ thesis work is considered outstanding and has impacted his field. The PhD thesis of Dr. _____ intended to contribute to the scientific knowledge within the field of the _____. The results achieved allowed to determine the _____. This study allowed the _____. The results were published in several high impact journals and conferences and cited by many colleagues. On the repository of the University of ▆▆▆▆, since ▆▆▆, the thesis had ▆▆▆ views and ▆▆▆ downloads. At ResearchGate the thesis had already more than ▆▆▆ reads (Please see exhibits E6.1 and E7).

The MSc Thesis of Dr. ▆▆▆ intended to contribute to scientific knowledge with the field of ▆▆▆▆▆▆▆. The results obtained allowed to improve the ▆▆▆▆▆ and to understand the ▆▆▆▆▆▆.

The results were published in several national and international conferences and cited by many colleagues. At Researchgate the thesis has already more than ▆▆▆ reads (Please see exhibits E6.2 and E7).

The bachelor's degree thesis of Dr. ▆▆▆ intended to contribute to scientific knowledge with the field of ▆▆▆▆▆▆.

This study presents ▆▆▆▆▆▆.

The results were published in several national and international conferences and cited by many colleagues. At ResearchGate the thesis has already more than ▆▆▆ reads (Please see exhibits E6.3 and E7).

Section 4: Dr. _____ seeks employment in the area of __________, an area of substantial intrinsic merit and national importance. His fundamental research can be considered beneficial to the United States due to the wide range of national applications.

Dr. _______ has a good history of working at academic institutions and on government funded projects developing the national and international scientific knowledge (Please see exhibits E4.1, E4.2., E4.3, E4.4). Dr. ______ work history is in an area of national interest that will help to _________ of the United States.

Dr. _______ outstanding accomplishments and exceptional abilities prove his capacity to perform at high level, and with that, impact the field as a whole to substantially greater degree than his U.S. Citizen counterparts having the same minimum qualifications. National interest would be adversely affected if a labor certification were required.

"Your resume is overqualified for even a top position in my company; however, at least to start, you will always be welcomed to join our team" (Please see exhibits E4.7, ________, Job offer at _____, ___, U.S.A.)

To summarize, the evidence presented by Dr. ⬚⬚⬚⬚⬚⬚ shows:

a) extraordinary ability (national award, member of ⬚⬚⬚⬚⬚⬚ in the field of ⬚⬚⬚⬚⬚⬚, published material about his work in media, national and international scientific publications, original scientific research of significance to the ⬚⬚⬚⬚⬚⬚ field, leading role on organizations with distinguished reputation, and a judge of others work);

b) he is one of the top experts in the field;

c) his work has enjoyed sustained acclaim (significant citations and article downloads);

d) he is in the US national interest.

"I had the opportunity to follow and discuss its research work, which came to provide relevant information for the ⬚⬚⬚⬚⬚⬚ from Country⬚⬚⬚⬚⬚⬚. Furthermore, the development of his work provided him advanced competences to assess the ⬚⬚⬚⬚⬚⬚.
Therefore, Dr. ⬚⬚⬚⬚⬚⬚ is a topmost researcher in his field, where he can have further contribution for the development of the state of art anywhere in the World. In particular, the U.S.A. have a large ⬚⬚⬚⬚⬚⬚, which will require ⬚⬚⬚⬚⬚⬚ in the next few years, and here Dr. ⬚⬚⬚⬚⬚⬚ can serve the national interests. For these reasons, I strongly support his application for permanent residency and recommend the government to accelerate its approval so that his essential scientific work can benefit the U.S.A." (Please see Exhibit E3.3, letter from Dr. ⬚⬚⬚⬚⬚⬚, University of ⬚⬚⬚⬚⬚⬚).

Table of Evidence vs Exhibits

Evidence	Exhibits
Evidence of receipt of lesser nationally or internationally recognized prizes or awards for excellence.	E4.1
Evidence of your membership in associations in the field which demand outstanding achievement of their members.	E4.2; E4.5; E4.6; E4.4
Evidence of published material about you in professional or major trade publications or other major media.	E7.5; E8.1
Evidence that you have been asked to judge the work of others, either individually or on a panel.	E5
Evidence of your original scientific, scholarly, artistic, athletic, or business-related contributions of major significance to the field.	E2; E3; E4.1; E4.2; E4.3; E6; E7; E8
Evidence of your authorship of scholarly articles in professional or major trade publications or other major media.	E7
Evidence that your work has been displayed at artistic exhibitions or showcases.	E8.2; E8.3; E7.3; E7.4; E7.5
Evidence of your performance of a leading or critical role in distinguished organizations.	E3; E4.1; E4.2; E4.3; E4.4; E5
Evidence that the petitioner is one of the small percentage of people who have risen to the very top of the field of endeavor.	E3; E4.1; E4.2; E4.3; E4.4; E4.5; E5; E7
Evidence that the petitioner has sustained national and international acclaim and that his achievements been recognized in the field of expertise.	E3; E5; E7
Evidence that the petitioner work is of national importance to the U.S.	E3; E4.7; E5.1

EB1A - Extraordinary Ability Petition – Dr. ▓▓▓▓▓▓▓▓▓▓▓▓

Exhibits index

E1. Curriculum Vitae

E2. Qualifications
    E2.1. PhD Certificate
    E2.2. Master Certificate
    E2.3. Bachelor's degree Certificate
    E2.4. Specialization field_____ Certificate
    E2.5. Specialization field_____ Certificate

E3. Reference letters
    E3.1. Dr. _____ – University of _____ – Country_____
    E3.2. Dr. _____ – University of _____ – Country_____
    E3.3. Dr. _____ – University of _____ – Country_____
    E3.4. Dr. _____ – University of _____ – Country_____
    E3.5. Dr. _____ – University of _____ – Country_____
    E3.6. Dr. _____ – Company_____ – Country_____
    E3.7. Dr. _____ – University of _____ – Country_____
    E3.8. Dr. _____ – University of _____ – Country_____

E4. Research & Civil Engineering Work
    E4.1. Post-Doc Research Grant - _____ – University of _____
    E4.2. Research member of the _____
    E4.3. PhD Research Grant – _____
    E4.4. Member of the _____
    E4.5. Member of the _____
    E4.6. Professional ID card from _____
    E4.7. Job Opportunity in U.S.A. – Company _____ – State_____

E5. Work as Judge & Reviewer
    E5.1. Scientific Reviewer of the _____
    E5.2. Member of the International Scientific Committee for the _____

E6. Thesis & Research reports
    E6.1. PhD thesis abstract, downloads and views from the University of _____
repository
    E6.2. MSc thesis abstract and reads from ResearchGate
    E6.3. Bachelor's degree thesis abstract and reads from ResearchGate
    E6.4. Post-doc research abstract & Report sample

E7. Publications & Citations
    E7.1. Google scholar citations
    E7.2. Publications & Citations report from ResearchGate
    E7.3. Publications on the University of _____ Repository
    E7.4. Publications on the University of _____ Repository
    E7.5. Book – _____ –
Publisher_____
    E7.6. Book – _____ –
Publisher_____

E7.7. Book Chapter – ██████████████████████ in
████████████████

retrofitting: learning from vernacular architecture – Publisher Taylor & Francis Group

E7.8. International Journal Article –
████████████████████████████████████

in _____ –

Publisher ████████████████████

E7.9. Samples of Published Articles

E8. Evidence of the scientific work being displayed

E8.1. Institution that promoted the presentation ████████████████████████

E8.2. Certificate of samples being presented at event

E8.3. Samples presented in international events

Please Note: If you want this template in word contact me at projectoinvicto@gmail.com

Made in United States
Troutdale, OR
04/18/2024